Informing the legislative debate since 1914

Navy Ship Names: Background for Congress

Ronald O'Rourke

Specialist in Naval Affairs

June 5, 2014

Congressional Research Service

7-5700

www.crs.gov

RS22478

Summary

Names for Navy ships traditionally have been chosen and announced by the Secretary of the Navy, under the direction of the President and in accordance with rules prescribed by Congress. Rules for giving certain types of names to certain types of Navy ships have evolved over time. There have been exceptions to the Navy's ship-naming rules, particularly for the purpose of naming a ship for a person when the rule for that type of ship would have called for it to be named for something else. Some observers in recent years have perceived a breakdown in, or corruption of, the rules for naming Navy ships. On July 13, 2012, the Navy submitted to Congress a 73-page report on the Navy's policies and practices for naming ships. The report, which was submitted in response to Section 1014 of the FY2012 National Defense Authorization Act (H.R. 1540/P.L. 112-81 of December 31, 2011), states: "Current ship naming policies and practices fall well within the historic spectrum of policies and practices for naming vessels of the Navy, and are altogether consistent with ship naming customs and traditions."

For ship types now being procured for the Navy, or recently procured for the Navy, naming rules can be summarized as follows:

- **Aircraft carriers** are generally named for past U.S. Presidents. Of the last 14, 10 were named for past U.S. Presidents, and 2 for Members of Congress.
- **Virginia (SSN-774) class attack submarines** are being named for states.
- **Destroyers** are named for deceased members of the Navy, Marine Corps, and Coast Guard, including Secretaries of the Navy.
- **Littoral Combat Ships (LCSs)** are being named for regionally important U.S. cities and communities.
- **Amphibious assault ships** are being named for important battles in which U.S. Marines played a prominent part, and for famous earlier U.S. Navy ships that were not named for battles.
- **San Antonio (LPD-17) class amphibious ships** are being named for major U.S. cities and communities, and cities and communities attacked on September 11, 2001.
- **Lewis and Clark (TAKE-1) class cargo and ammunition ships** were named for famous American explorers, trailblazers, and pioneers.
- **Mobile Landing Platform (MLP) ships/Afloat Forward Staging Bases (AFSBs)** are being named for famous names or places of historical significance to U.S. Marines.

The Navy historically has only rarely named ships for living persons. Since 1973, at least 15 U.S. military ships have been named for persons who were living at the time the name was announced. Members of the public are sometimes interested in having Navy ships named for their own states or cities, for older U.S. Navy ships (particularly those on which they or their relatives served), for battles in which they or their relatives participated, or for people they admire.

Congress has long maintained an interest in how Navy ships are named, and has influenced the naming of certain Navy ships. The Navy suggests that congressional offices wishing to express support for proposals to name a Navy ship for a specific person, place, or thing contact the office of the Secretary of the Navy to make their support known. Congress may also pass legislation relating to ship names. Measures passed by Congress in recent years regarding Navy ship names have all been sense-of-the-Congress provisions.

Contents

Tables

Appendixes

Contacts

Background

July 2012 Navy Report to Congress

On July 13, 2012, the Navy submitted to Congress a 73-page report on the Navy's policies and practices for naming ships.[1] The report was submitted in response to Section 1014 of the FY2012 National Defense Authorization Act (H.R. 1540/P.L. 112-81 of December 31, 2011). (For the text of Section 1024, see the entry for H.R. 1540/P.L. 112-81 in **Appendix B**.) The executive summary of the Navy's report is reprinted here as **Appendix A**.[2]

Authority for Naming Ships

Names for Navy ships traditionally have been chosen and announced by the Secretary of the Navy, under the direction of the President and in accordance with rules prescribed by Congress. For most of the 19th century, U.S. law included language explicitly assigning the Secretary of the Navy the task of naming new Navy ships.[3] The reference to the Secretary of the Navy disappeared from the U.S. Code in 1925.[4] The code today (10 U.S.C. §7292) is silent on the issue of who has the authority to name new Navy ships,[5] but the Secretary of the Navy arguably retains implicit authority, given the location of Section 7292 in subtitle C of Title 10, which covers the Navy and Marine Corps.

---

[1] Department of the Navy, *A Report on Policies and Practices of the U.S. Navy for Naming the Vessels of the Navy*, undated but transmitted to Congress with cover letters dated July 13, 2012, 73 pp. As of November 19, 2013, the report was posted at http://www history navy mil/download/Shipnamingreport.pdf.

[2] For an article providing a critical perspective on the Navy's report, see Norman Polmar, "Report on Ship Naming Falls Short," *Seapower*, October 2012: 6-7.

[3] A law approved in 1819 (Res. of March 3, 1819, §1, 3 Stat. 538, No. 7) stated "That all of the ships of the navy of the United States, now building, or hereafter to be built, shall be named by the Secretary of the Navy, under the direction of the President of the United States" in accordance with rules specifying that ships of the first class were to be named after states of the Union, and second and third class ships were to be named, respectively, after rivers and principal cities and towns. A law approved in 1858 (Act of June 12, 1858, c. 153, §5, 11 Stat. 319) provided a similar rule for "steamships of the navy," except that third-class vessels (those with fewer than twenty guns) were to be named by the Secretary of the Navy as the President may direct, taking care that no two vessels in the Navy shall bear the same name." §1531 of the Revised Statutes of 1873-1874, citing the 1819 and 1858 laws, states: "The vessels of the Navy shall be named by the Secretary of the Navy, under the direction of the President" in accordance with rules similar to those above, varying slightly depending on whether the vessel was a sailing ship or a steamship. In 1898, Congress passed a law (Act of May 4, 1898, c. 234, 30 Stat. 390 [appropriations for the naval services]) prescribing rules for the naming of "first-class battle ships and monitors," which specified that these were to be named after States and "shall not be named for any city, place, or persons until the names of the States, shall have been exhausted." The provision did not explicitly state whose duty it would be to assign names to vessels. Congress repealed this provision in 1908 as it pertained to monitors, permitting those vessels to be named "as the President may direct." (Act of May 13, 1908, c. 166, 35 Stat. 159.)

[4] The reference to the Secretary of the Navy found in §1531 of the Revised Statutes of 1873-1874 (see previous footnote) is absent from the U.S. Code of 1925, which covers Navy vessel names in Title 34, §461-463.

[5] 34 U.S.C. §461-463 of the 1925 U.S. Code (see previous footnote) were later recodified as 10 U.S.C. §7292. 10 U.S.C. §7292 provides that battleships are to be "named for a State. However, if the names of all the States are in use, a battleship may be named for a city, place, or person." It specifically authorizes the Secretary of the Navy to "change the name of any vessel bought for the Navy," §7292(c), but does not explicitly assign responsibility for ensuring that no two vessels have the same name, §7292(a), or for naming battleships, §7292(b).

Navy's Process for Selecting Names

In discussing its name-selection process, the Naval History and Heritage Command—the Navy's in-house office of professional historians—cites the above-mentioned laws and states:

> As with many other things, the procedures and practices involved in Navy ship naming are as much, if not more, products of evolution and tradition than of legislation. As we have seen, the names for new ships are personally decided by the Secretary of the Navy. The Secretary can rely on many sources to help him reach his decisions. Each year, the Naval Historical Center compiles primary and alternate ship name recommendations and forwards these to the Chief of Naval Operations by way of the chain of command. These recommendations are the result of research into the history of the Navy and by suggestions submitted by service members, Navy veterans, and the public. Ship name source records at the Historical Center reflect the wide variety of name sources that have been used in the past, particularly since World War I. Ship name recommendations are conditioned by such factors as the name categories for ship types now being built, as approved by the Secretary of the Navy; the distribution of geographic names of ships of the Fleet; names borne by previous ships which distinguished themselves in service; names recommended by individuals and groups; and names of naval leaders, national figures, and deceased members of the Navy and Marine Corps who have been honored for heroism in war or for extraordinary achievement in peace.
>
> In its final form, after consideration at the various levels of command, the Chief of Naval Operations signs the memorandum recommending names for the current year's building program and sends it to the Secretary of the Navy. The Secretary considers these nominations, along with others he receives as well as his own thoughts in this matter. At appropriate times, he selects names for specific ships and announces them.
>
> While there is no set time for assigning a name, it is customarily done before the ship is christened. The ship's sponsor—the person who will christen the ship—is also selected and invited by the Secretary. In the case of ships named for individuals, an effort is made to identify the eldest living direct female descendant of that individual to perform the role of ship's sponsor. For ships with other name sources, it is customary to honor the wives of senior naval officers or public officials.[6]

The July 2012 Navy report to Congress states:

> Once a type/class naming convention [i.e., a general rule or guideline for how ships of a certain type or class are to be named] is established, Secretaries can rely on many sources to help in the final selection of a ship name. For example, sitting Secretaries can solicit ideas and recommendations from either the Chief of Naval Operations (CNO) or the Commandant of the Marine Corps (CMC), or both. They can also task the Naval Heritage and History Command to compile primary and alternate ship name recommendations that are the result of research into the history of the Navy's battle force or particular ship names. Secretaries also routinely receive formal suggestions for ship names from concerned citizens, active and retired service members, or members of Congress. Finally, Congress can enact provisions in Public Law that express the sense of the entire body about new ship naming conventions or specific ship names. Regardless of the origin of the recommendations, however, the final selection of a ship's name is the Secretary's to make, informed and guided by his own thoughts, counsel, and preferences. At the appropriate time—normally sometime after the

---

[6] Naval History and Heritage Command, "Ship Naming in the United States Navy," accessed online on February 10, 2014, at http://www history navy.mil/faqs/faq63-1 htm.

ship has been either authorized or appropriated by Congress and before its keel laying or christening—the Secretary records his decision with a formal naming announcement.[7]

Naming Rules for Ship Types

Evolution Over Time

Rules for giving certain types of names to certain types of Navy ships have evolved over time. Attack submarines, for example, were once named for fish, then later for cities, and most recently for states, while cruisers were once named for cities, then later for states,[8] and most recently for battles. State names, to cite another example, were given to battleships, then later to nuclear-powered cruisers and ballistic missile submarines, and are now being given to attack submarines.

The Naval History and Heritage Command states that "While the Navy has attempted to be systematic in naming its ships, like all institutions it has been subject to evolutionary change, and the name sources of the Navy's ships have not been immune to this change.... How will the Navy name its ships in the future? It seems safe to say that the evolutionary process of the past will continue; as the Fleet itself changes, so will the names given to its ships."[9] The July 2012 Navy report to Congress states that "US Navy ship-naming policies, practices, and 'traditions' are not fixed; they evolve constantly over time."[10] The report also states that "Just as [ship] type naming conventions change over time to accommodate technological change as well as choices made by Secretaries, they also change over time as every Secretary makes their own interpretation of the original naming convention."[11]

---

[7] Department of the Navy, *A Report on Policies and Practices of the U.S. Navy for Naming the Vessels of the Navy*, undated but transmitted to Congress with cover letters dated July 13, 2012, p. 3. At the end of this quoted passage, there is a footnote (number 3) that states:

> Although there is no hard and fast rule, Secretaries most often name a ship after Congress has appropriated funds for its construction or approved its future construction in some way—such as authorization of either block buys or multi-year procurements of a specific number of ships. There are special cases, however, when Secretaries use their discretion to name ships before formal Congressional approval, such as when Secretary John Lehman announced the namesake for a new class of Aegis guided missile destroyers would be Admiral Arleigh Burke, several years before the ship was either authorized or appropriated.

In connection with the above passage, the lead ship of the DDG-51 class of destroyers was named for Arleigh Burke on November 5, 1982, about two years before the ship was authorized and fully funded. (Congress authorized the ship in the FY1985 National Defense Authorization Act [H.R. 5167/P.L. 98-525 of October 19, 1984], and fully funded the ship in H.J.Res. 648/P.L. 98-473 of October 12, 1984, a joint resolution making continuing appropriations for the fiscal year 1985, and for other purposes.)

[8] Cruisers named for states were nuclear-powered cruisers.

[9] Naval History and Heritage Command, "Ship Naming in the United States Navy," accessed online on February 10, 2014, at http://www history navy mil/faqs/faq63-1 htm.

[10] Department of the Navy, *A Report on Policies and Practices of the U.S. Navy for Naming the Vessels of the Navy*, undated but transmitted to Congress with cover letters dated July 13, 2012, p. 10.

[11] Department of the Navy, *A Report on Policies and Practices of the U.S. Navy for Naming the Vessels of the Navy*, undated but transmitted to Congress with cover letters dated July 13, 2012, p. 25.

Exceptions

There have been numerous exceptions to the Navy's ship-naming rules, particularly for the purpose of naming a ship for a person when the rule for that type of ship would have called for it to be named for something else.[12] The July 2012 report to Congress cites exceptions to ship naming rules dating back to the earliest days of the republic, and states that "a Secretary's discretion to make exceptions to ship-naming conventions is one of the Navy's oldest ship-naming traditions."[13] The report argues that exceptions made for the purpose of naming ships for Presidents or Members of Congress have occurred frequently enough that, rather than being exceptions, they constitute a "special cross-type naming convention" for Presidents and Members of Congress.[14] (This CRS report continues to note, as exceptions to basic class naming rules, instances where ships other than aircraft carriers have been named for Presidents or Members of Congress.)

Some observers in recent years have perceived a breakdown in, or corruption of, the rules for naming Navy ships.[15] Such observers might cite, for example, the three-ship Seawolf (SSN-21)

---

[12] Ohio (SSBN-726) class ballistic missile submarines, for example, were named for states, but one (SSBN-730) was named for Senator Henry "Scoop" Jackson of Washington, who died in office in 1983. Los Angeles (SSN-688) class attack submarines were named for cities, but one (SSN-709) was named for Admiral Hyman G. Rickover, the longtime director of the Navy's nuclear propulsion program. Ticonderoga (CG-47) class cruisers were named for battles, but one (CG-51) was named for Thomas S. Gates, a former Secretary of the Navy and Secretary of Defense.

[13] Department of the Navy, *A Report on Policies and Practices of the U.S. Navy for Naming the Vessels of the Navy*, undated but transmitted to Congress with cover letters dated July 13, 2012, p. 7.

[14] The report states that

> the decision of the [Navy's 1969] Riera Panel [on Navy ship names] to remove members of Congress from the destroyer naming convention resulted in a now four-decade old, *bipartisan* practice of honoring members of Congress with long records of support to the US military with ships names selected and spread across a variety of ship types and classes. Orthodox Traditionalists decry this development as an unwarranted intrusion of "politics" in Navy ship naming practice. But this is a selective interpretation of the historical record. Secretaries of the Navy have been naming ships for members of Congress *for nearly a century* in order to honor those extraordinary elected leaders who have helped to make the Navy-Marine Corps Team the most powerful naval force in history.

> Like many Pragmatic Secretaries of the Navy before him, Secretary [of the Navy Ray] Mabus endorses and subscribes to this special naming convention....

> Objections to Secretary Mabus's decision to name a ship in honor of Congressman Murtha generally fall into one of four categories. The first are Orthodox Traditionalists who naturally complain that his selection represents a corruption of the LPD 17 naming convention. However, as outlined above, the choice is perfectly consistent with the special cross-type naming convention that honors Legislative Branch members who have been closely identified with military and naval affairs, which has been endorsed by Secretaries from both parties and Congress....

> In summary, while USS John P. Murtha represents an exception to the *established* LPD 17 [amphibious ship] class naming convention, it is completely consistent with the *special* cross-type naming convention for honoring famous American elected leaders, including both Presidents and members of Congress with records of long-term service and support to the US armed forces.

> (Department of the Navy, *A Report on Policies and Practices of the U.S. Navy for Naming the Vessels of the Navy*, undated but transmitted to Congress with cover letters dated July 13, 2012, pp. 28-30. Italics as in original. See also pp. 37, 41, 42, 44, 47, 68, and 73.)

[15] See, for example, Donald R. Bouchoux, "The Name Game," *U.S. Naval Institute Proceedings*, March 2000: 110-111; Norman Polmar, "Misnaming Aircraft Carriers," *U.S. Naval Institute Proceedings*, September 2006: 30-31; Norman Polmar, "Misnaming Navy Ships (Again)," *U.S. Naval Institute Proceedings*, February 2009: 89; and Norman Polmar, "There's a Lot in a Name," *U.S. Naval Institute Proceedings*, April 2012: 88-89.

---

class of attack submarines—*Seawolf* (SSN-21), *Connecticut* (SSN-22), and *Jimmy Carter* (SSN-23)—which were named for a fish, a state, and a President, respectively, reflecting no apparent class naming rule.[16] The July 2012 Navy report to Congress states: "Current ship naming policies and practices fall well within the historic spectrum of policies and practices for naming vessels of the Navy, and are altogether consistent with ship naming customs and traditions."[17]

Rules for Ship Types Now Being Procured

For ship types now being procured for the Navy, or recently procured for the Navy, naming rules (and exceptions thereto) are summarized below. The July 2012 Navy report to Congress discusses current naming rules (and exceptions thereto) at length.

Aircraft Carriers

The July 2012 Navy report to Congress states that "while carrier names are still 'individually considered,' they are now generally named in honor of past US Presidents."[18] Of the 14 most recently named aircraft carriers (those with hull numbers 67 through 80), 10 have been named for U.S. Presidents and 2 for Members of Congress.

The Navy on May 29, 2011, announced that the aircraft carrier CVN-79 would be named for President John F. Kennedy.[19]

The Navy on December 1, 2012, announced that the aircraft carrier CVN-80 would be named *Enterprise*. The Navy made the announcement on the same day that it deactivated the 51-year-old aircraft carrier CVN-65, also named *Enterprise*.[20] CVN-65 was the eighth Navy ship named *Enterprise*; CVN-80 is to be the ninth. CVN-80 is currently scheduled for procurement in FY2018, a budget that Congress is to consider in 2017. Naming a ship approximately five years before it is scheduled to be authorized is unusual. The closest comparable case, at least from recent years, may be the destroyer *Zumwalt* (DDG-1000), whose name was announced by President Bill Clinton on July 4, 2000.[21] At the time of that announcement, Congress was considering the Navy's proposed FY2001 budget, under which DDG-1000 was scheduled for authorization in FY2005, a budget that Congress would consider in 2004, which was then about

---

[16] See, for example, Norman Polmar, "There's a Lot in a Name," *U.S. Naval Institute Proceedings*, April 2012: 88-89, which characterizes the naming of the Seawolf class as a "fiasco." For the Navy's discussion of the Seawolf class names, see Department of the Navy, *A Report on Policies and Practices of the U.S. Navy for Naming the Vessels of the Navy*, undated but transmitted to Congress with cover letters dated July 13, 2012, pp. 46-47.

[17] Department of the Navy, *A Report on Policies and Practices of the U.S. Navy for Naming the Vessels of the Navy*, undated but transmitted to Congress with cover letters dated July 13, 2012, p. iii.

[18] Department of the Navy, *A Report on Policies and Practices of the U.S. Navy for Naming the Vessels of the Navy*, undated but transmitted to Congress with cover letters dated July 13, 2012, p. 37.

[19] DOD News Release No. 449-11, May 29, 2011, entitled "Navy Names Next Aircraft Carrier USS John F. Kennedy," accessed July 27, 2012, at http://www.defense.gov/releases/release.aspx?releaseid=14523. CVN-79 will be the second aircraft carrier named for Kennedy. The first, CV-67, was the last conventionally powered carrier procured for the Navy. CV-67 was procured in FY1963, entered service in 1968, and was decommissioned in 2007.

[20] "Enterprise, Navy's First Nuclear-Powered Aircraft Carrier, Inactivated," *Navy News Service*, December 1, 2012; Hugh Lessig, "Navy Retires One Enterprise, Will Welcome Another," *Newport News Daily Press*, December 2, 2012.

[21] In response to a request from CRS for examples in recent years of ships that were named well in advance of when they were authorized, the Navy on December 7, 2012, sent an email citing the case of the *Zumwalt* and two other ships (DDG-51 and LPD-17) whose naming lead times were substantially less than that of the *Zumwalt*.

---

four years in the future.[22] Congress has not yet provided any procurement or advance procurement (AP) funding for CVN-80 (the initial increment of AP funding is scheduled for FY2016, a budget that Congress will consider in 2015), and CVN-80 is not covered under a multiyear procurement (MYP) contract or block buy contract that would represent a fairly strong government commitment to the eventual procurement of the ship.[23] If CVN-80, like most Navy ships, had instead been named at about the time of its scheduled authorization, or later, it might have been named by the Secretary of the Navy who will serve under the President to be elected in November 2016. The July 2012 Navy report to Congress states that

> Secretary [of the Navy Ray] Mabus values the ability to consider [aircraft] carrier names on an individual, case-by-case basis, for two reasons. First, it will allow a future Secretary to name a future fleet aircraft carrier for someone or something other than a former President. Indeed, Secretary Mabus has a particular name in mind. With the scheduled decommissioning of USS Enterprise (CVN 65), perhaps the most famous ship name in US Navy history besides USS Constitution will be removed from the Naval Vessel Register. Secretary Mabus believes this circumstance could be remedied by bestowing the Enterprise's storied name on a future carrier.[24]

In addition, if CVN-80 had been named at about the time of its scheduled authorization, or later, the 113th and 114th Congresses would have had an opportunity to express views concerning potential names for the ship.

Prior to the naming of CVN-80, the most recent carrier that was not named for a President or Member of Congress was the second of the 14 most recently named carriers, *Nimitz* (CVN-68), which was procured in FY1967.[25]

Attack Submarines

Virginia (SSN-774) class attack submarines are being named for states. An exception occurred on January 8, 2009, when then-Secretary of the Navy Donald Winter announced that SSN-785, the 12th ship in the class, would be named for former Senator John Warner.[26]

---

[22] The FY2006 budget submission subsequently deferred the scheduled procurement of DDG-1000 to FY2007. DDG-1000 and the second ship in the class, DDG-1001, were procured in FY2007 using split funding (i.e., two-year incremental funding) in FY2007 and FY2008.

[23] For more on MYP and block buy contracting, see CRS Report R41909, *Multiyear Procurement (MYP) and Block Buy Contracting in Defense Acquisition: Background and Issues for Congress*, by Ronald O'Rourke and Moshe Schwartz.

[24] Department of the Navy, *A Report on Policies and Practices of the U.S. Navy for Naming the Vessels of the Navy*, undated but transmitted to Congress with cover letters dated July 13, 2012, p. 37. See also the discussion in footnote 7.

[25] CVN-68 was named for Fleet Admiral Chester Nimitz, a five-star admiral who commanded U.S. and allied forces in the Pacific in World War II. Nimitz died in 1966, the same year that Congress considered the FY1967 defense budget that funded the procurement of CVN-68.

[26] DOD News Release No. 016-09, January 8, 2009, entitled "Navy Names Virginia Class Submarine USS John Warner," accessed July 27, 2012, at http://www.defense.gov/releases/release.aspx?releaseid=12431. Warner served as a sailor in World War II, as a Marine in the Korean War, as Under Secretary of the Navy in 1969-1972, and as Secretary of the Navy in 1972-1974. Warner served as a Senator from January 2, 1979, to January 3, 2009. He was a longtime Member of the Senate Armed Services Committee, and was for several years the chairman of that committee. Winter's January 8, 2009, announcement assigned a name to SSN-785 eleven months before the ship was fully funded. (The ship was fully funded by the FY2010 Department of Defense (DOD) appropriations act [H.R. 3326/P.L. 111-118], which was signed into law on December 19, 2009.) Naming a ship almost a year before it is funded is unusual. Winter stepped down as Secretary of the Navy on March 13, 2009. If SSN-785 had not been named for Warner, the 111th Congress (continued...)

As of June 5, 2014, the Navy had posted names for Virginia-class boats up through SSN-791, the second of the two Virginia-class boats procured in FY2013, and had not yet posted names for SSN-792 and SSN-793, the two Virginia-class boats procured in FY2014.

Destroyers

Destroyers traditionally have been named for famous U.S. naval leaders and distinguished heroes. The July 2012 Navy report to Congress discusses this tradition and states more specifically that destroyers are being named for deceased members of the Navy, Marine Corps, and Coast Guard, including Secretaries of the Navy. An exception occurred on May 7, 2012, when the Navy announced that it was naming DDG-116, an Arleigh Burke (DDG-51) class destroyer, for a living person, Thomas Hudner.[27] Another exception occurred on May 23, 2013, when the Navy announced that it was naming DDG-117, another DDG-51 class destroyer, for a living person, Paul Ignatius. The Navy on May 23, 2013, also announced that it was naming DDG-118, another DDG-51 class destroyer, for the late Senator Daniel Inouye, who died on December 17, 2012.[28]

As of June 5, 2014, the Navy had posted names for DDG-51 class destroyers up through DDG-118, the second of three DDG-51s procured in FY2013, and had not yet posted names for DDG-120, the third DDG-51 procured in FY2013, and DDG-119, the one DDG-51 procured in FY2014.

Littoral Combat Ships (LCSs)

Littoral Combat Ships (LCSs) were at first named for U.S. mid-tier cities, small towns, and other U.S. communities.[29] The naming convention for LCSs was later adjusted to regionally important U.S. cities and communities. An exception occurred on February 10, 2012, when the Navy announced that it was naming LCS-10 for former Representative Gabrielle Giffords.[30]

As of June 5, 2014, the Navy had posted names for LCSs up through LCS-17, the first of four LCSs procured in FY2014, and had not yet posted names for LCSs 18 through 20, the other three LCSs procured in FY2014.

(...continued)

might have had an opportunity to consider whether CVN-79, the next Ford-class carrier, should be named for Warner. One observer has argued that in light of Warner's record and past traditions for naming Navy ships, "he should be honored by an aircraft carrier (two CVNs [nuclear-powered aircraft carriers] have been named for Members of Congress) or possibly the lead ship for the planned class of CG(X) cruisers—but not a submarine." (Norman Polmar, "Misnaming Navy Ships (Again)," *U.S. Naval Institute Proceedings*, February 2009: 89.)

[27] DOD News Release No. 352-12, May 7, 2012, entitled "Secretary of the Navy Announces DDG 116 to Be Named Thomas Hudner," accessed July 27, 2012, at http://www.defense.gov/releases/release.aspx?releaseid=15252.

[28] DOD News Release No. 361-13, May 23, 2013, entitled "Navy Names Next Two Destroyers," accessed May 28, 2013, at http://www.defense.gov/releases/release.aspx?releaseid=16032.

[29] The Navy named LCS-1 and LCS-2 *Freedom* and *Independence*, respectively, after multiple U.S. cities with these names.

[30] DOD News Release No. 096-12, February 10, 2012, entitled "Navy Names Littoral Combat Ship Gabrielle Giffords," accessed July 27, 2012, at http://www.defense.gov/releases/release.aspx?releaseid=15055. For the Navy's discussion of this naming choice, see Department of the Navy, *A Report on Policies and Practices of the U.S. Navy for Naming the Vessels of the Navy*, undated but transmitted to Congress with cover letters dated July 13, 2012, pp. 33-34.

LHA-6 Class Amphibious Assault Ships

Amphibious assault ships are being named for important battles in which U.S. Marines played a prominent part, and for famous earlier U.S. Navy ships that were not named for battles. The Navy announced on June 27, 2008, that the first LHA-6 class amphibious assault ship would be named *America*, a name previously used for an aircraft carrier (CV-66) that served in the Navy from 1965 to 1996. The Navy announced on May 4, 2012, that LHA-7, the second ship in the class, would be named *Tripoli*, the location of famous Marine battles in the First Barbary War.[31] The Navy reaffirmed this name selection with a more formal announcement on May 30, 2014.[32]

LPD-17 Class Amphibious Ships

San Antonio (LPD-17) class amphibious ships are being named for major U.S. cities and communities (with major being defined as being one of the top three population centers in a state), and cities and communities attacked on September 11, 2001. An exception occurred on April 23, 2010, when the Navy announced that it was naming LPD-26, the 10th ship in the class, for the late Representative John P. Murtha.[33]

TAKE-1 Class Dry Cargo and Ammunition Ships

The Navy's 14 Lewis and Clark (TAKE-1) class cargo and ammunition ships were named for famous American explorers, trailblazers, and pioneers. The Navy announced on October 9, 2009, that the 13th ship in the class was being named for the civil rights activist Medgar Evers.[34] The Navy announced on May 18, 2011, that the 14th ship in the class would be named for civil rights activist Cesar Chavez.[35]

Joint High Speed Vessels (JHSVs)

Joint High Speed Vessels (JHSVs), which until May 2011 were being procured by the Army as well as by the Navy, were at first named for American traits and values. In December 2009, the

---

[31] DOD News Release No. 347-12, May 4, 2012, entitled "Secretary of the Navy Announces LHA 7 Will Be Named USS Tripoli," accessed July 27, 2012, at http://www.defense.gov/releases/release.aspx?releaseid=15247. The name Tripoli was previously used for an amphibious assault ship (LPH-10) that served in the Navy from 1966 to 1995, and for an escort carrier (CVE-64) that served in the Navy from 1943 to 1946.

[32] "SECNAV Formally Names USS Tripoli," *Navy News Service*, June 2, 2014.

[33] DOD News Release No. 329-10, April 23, 2010, entitled "Navy Names Amphibious Ship For Congressman John Murtha," accessed July 27, 2012, at http://www.defense.gov/releases/release.aspx?releaseid=13478. For the Navy's discussion of this naming choice, see Department of the Navy, *A Report on Policies and Practices of the U.S. Navy for Naming the Vessels of the Navy*, undated but transmitted to Congress with cover letters dated July 13, 2012, pp. 28-30.

[34] DOD News Release No. 788-09, October 9, 2009, entitled "Navy Names Ship After Civil Rights Activist Medgar Evers," accessed July 27, 2012, at http://www.defense.gov/releases/release.aspx?releaseid=13036. For the Navy's discussion of this naming choice, see Department of the Navy, *A Report on Policies and Practices of the U.S. Navy for Naming the Vessels of the Navy*, undated but transmitted to Congress with cover letters dated July 13, 2012, pp. 21-22.

[35] DOD News Release No. 420-11, May 18, 2011, entitled "Navy Names Ship For Civil Rights Activist Cesar Chavez," accessed July 27, 2012, at http://www.defense.gov/releases/release.aspx?releaseid=14504. For the Navy's discussion of this naming choice, see Department of the Navy, *A Report on Policies and Practices of the U.S. Navy for Naming the Vessels of the Navy*, undated but transmitted to Congress with cover letters dated July 13, 2012, pp. 22-24.

---

naming convention for JHSVs was changed to small U.S. cities. At some point between December 2010 and October 2011, it was adjusted to small U.S. cities and counties.[36]

Mobile Landing Platform (MLP) Ships/Afloat Forward Staging Bases (AFSBs)

The Navy's four planned Mobile Landing Platform (MLP) ships—the last two of which the Navy wants to build to a modified configuration so that they would serve as Afloat Forward Staging Bases (AFSBs)—are being named for famous names or places of historical significance to U.S. Marines. On January 4, 2012, the Secretary of the Navy announced that the first three MLPs were being named *Montford Point*, *John Glenn*, and *Lewis B. Puller*.[37]

State Names That Have Not Been Used in a Long Time

It has been a long time since ships named for certain states were last in commissioned service with the Navy as combat assets. While there is no rule requiring the Navy, in selecting state names for ships, to choose states for which the most time has passed since a ship named for the state has been in commissioned service with the Navy as a combat asset, advocates of naming a ship for a certain state may choose to point out, among other things, the length of time that has transpired since a ship named for the state has been in commissioned service with the Navy as a combat asset.

In its announcement of April 13, 2012, that the Navy was naming the Virginia class attack submarines SSNs 786 through 790 for Illinois, Washington, Colorado, Indiana, and South Dakota, respectively, the Department of Defense stated, "None of the five states has had a ship named for it for more than 49 years. The most recent to serve was the battleship Indiana, which was decommissioned in October 1963."[38] The July 2012 Navy report to Congress states: "Before deciding on which names to select [for the five submarines], Secretary [of the Navy Ray] Mabus asked for a list of State names that had been absent the longest from the US Naval Register.... "[39]

In its announcement of November 19, 2012, that the Navy was naming the Virginia class attack submarine SSN-791 for Delaware, the Department of Defense quoted Secretary Mabus as saying, "It has been too long since there has been a USS Delaware in the fleet.... "[40]

A CRS review of online Navy ship name records[41] suggests that there is a small handful of states for which the most time—roughly 90 years—has passed since a ship named for the state has been

---

[36] Department of the Navy, *A Report on Policies and Practices of the U.S. Navy for Naming the Vessels of the Navy*, undated but transmitted to Congress with cover letters dated July 13, 2012, pp. 18-19.

[37] DOD News Release No. 007-12, January 4, 2012, entitled "Navy Names First Three Landing Platform Ships," accessed January 6, 2012, at http://www.defense.gov/releases/release.aspx?releaseid=14991. For the Navy's discussion of these naming choices, see Department of the Navy, *A Report on Policies and Practices of the U.S. Navy for Naming the Vessels of the Navy*, undated but transmitted to Congress with cover letters dated July 13, 2012, pp. 39-40.

[38] DOD News Release No. 264-12, April 13, 2012, entitled "Navy Names Five New Submarines," accessed April 25, 2012, at http://www.defense.gov/releases/release.aspx?releaseid=15180.

[39] Department of the Navy, *A Report on Policies and Practices of the U.S. Navy for Naming the Vessels of the Navy*, undated but transmitted to Congress with cover letters dated July 13, 2012, p. 48.

[40] DOD News Release No. 914-12, November 19, 2012, entitled "Secretary of the Navy Ray Mabus Names the Next Virginia-Class Submarine USS Delaware with Dr. Jill Biden as the Sponsor," accessed November 19, 2012, at http://www.defense.gov/releases/release.aspx?releaseid=15694.

---

in commissioned service with the Navy as a combat asset, and for which no ship by that name is currently under construction. These states appear to include, but may not be limited to, the following, which are presented in alphabetical order: Kansas, Montana, Oregon, and Vermont. (This group also included Illinois and Delaware until the above-noted Navy naming announcements of April 13, 2012, and November 19, 2012, respectively.) There are additional states for which lesser—but still substantial—amounts of time have passed since a ship named for the state has been in commissioned service with the Navy as a combat asset, and for which no ship by that name is currently under construction.

Ships Named for Living Persons

The Navy historically has only rarely named ships for living persons. The Navy stated in February 2012 that

> The Navy named several ships for living people (ex. George Washington, Ben Franklin, etc.) in the early years of our Republic. The Naval History and Heritage Command (NHHC) believes that the last ship to be named by the Navy in honor of a living person prior to [the aircraft carrier] CARL VINSON (CVN-70) was the brig JEFFERSON (launched in April 1814). Between 1814 and November 18, 1973, when President Nixon announced the naming of CARL VINSON,[42] NHHC does not believe that any ships had been named for a living person by the Navy as NHHC does not have records that would indicate such.[43]

The July 2012 Navy report to Congress, noting a case from 1900 that was not included in the above passage, states that

> the practice of naming ships in honor of deserving Americans or naval leaders while they are still alive can be traced all the way back to the Revolutionary War. At the time, with little established history or tradition, the young Continental Navy looked to honor those who were fighting so hard to earn America's freedom. Consequently, George Washington had no less than five ships named for him before his death; John Adams and James Madison, three apiece; John Hancock, two; and Benjamin Franklin, one.
>
> The practice of naming ships after living persons was relatively commonplace up through 1814, when a US Navy brig was named in honor of Thomas Jefferson. However, after the War of 1812, with the US Navy older and more established, and with the list of famous Americans and notable naval heroes growing ever longer, the practice of naming ships after living persons fell into disuse. Indeed, the only exception over the next 150 years came in 1900, when the Navy purchased its first submarine from its still living inventor, John Philip Holland, and Secretary of the Navy John D. Long named her USS Holland (SS 1) in his honor....
>
> [In the early 1970s], however, Department of the Navy leaders were considering the name for CVN 70. Secretary of the Navy John Warner knew the 93rd Congress had introduced no

---

(...continued)

[41] The online records reviewed by CRS were the Naval Vessel Register (http://www nvr navy mil/) and the Dictionary of American Naval Fighting Ships (http://www history navy mil/danfs/index.html).

[42] Although President Nixon announced on November 18, 1973 that CVN-70 would be named for Carl Vinson, as shown in **Table 1**, the name apparently was officially given to the ship on January 18, 1974.

[43] Navy information paper dated February 28, 2012, provided to CRS by Navy Office of Legislative Affairs, March 1, 2012.

less than three bills or amendments (none enacted) urging that CVN 70 be named for in honor of Carl Vinson, who served in the House for 50 years and was known as the "Father of the Two-Ocean Navy." Although Secretary Warner felt Congressman Vinson was more than worthy of a ship name, the former Congressman was still alive. Naming a ship for this giant of naval affairs would therefore violate a 160-year old tradition. After considering the pros and cons of doing so, Secretary Warner asked President Richard Nixon's approval to name CVN 70 for the 90-year old statesman. President Nixon readily agreed. Indeed, he personally announced the decision on January 18, 1974....

In hindsight, rather than this decision being a rare exception, it signaled a return to the Continental Navy tradition of occasionally honoring famous living persons with a ship name. Since then, and before the appointment of current Secretary of the Navy Ray Mabus, Secretaries of the Navy have occasionally chosen to follow this new, "old tradition," naming ships in honor of still living former Presidents Jimmy Carter, Ronald Reagan, George H.W. Bush, and Gerald R. Ford; Secretary of the Navy Paul Nitze; Navy Admirals Hyman G. Rickover, Arleigh Burke, and Wayne E. Meyer; Senators John C. Stennis and John Warner; and famous entertainer Bob Hope. Moreover, it is important to note that three of these well-known Americans—Gerald R. Ford, John C. Stennis, and Bob Hope—were so honored after Congress enacted provisions in Public Laws urging the Navy to do so. By its own actions, then, Congress has acknowledged the practice of occasionally naming ships for living persons, if not outright approved of it.

In other words, while naming ships after living persons remains a relatively rare occurrence—about three per decade since 1970—it is now an accepted but sparingly used practice for Pragmatic Secretaries [of the Navy] of both parties. For them, occasionally honoring an especially deserving member of Congress, US naval leader, or famous American with a ship name so that they might end their days on earth knowing that their life's work is both recognized and honored by America's Navy-Marine Corps Team, and that their spirit will accompany and inspire the Team in battle, is sometimes exactly the right thing to do.[44]

As shown in **Table 1**, since the naming of CVN-70 for Carl Vinson in 1974, at least 15 U.S. military ships have been named for persons who were living at the time the name was announced. Four of the 15 have been announced since January 2012.

---

[44] Department of the Navy, *A Report on Policies and Practices of the U.S. Navy for Naming the Vessels of the Navy*, undated but transmitted to Congress with cover letters dated July 13, 2012, pp. 7-9.

Table 1. Ships Since 1973 Named for Persons Who Were Living at the Time

Ship type	Hull number	Ship name	Date name announced	Age of person when name was announced	Fiscal year ship was procured	Year ship entered or is to enter service
Aircraft carrier	CVN-70	*Carl Vinson*	1/18/1974	90	FY1974	1982
Attack submarine	SSN-709	*Hyman G. Rickover*	5/9/1983	83	FY1974	1984
Destroyer	DDG-51	*Arleigh Burke*	11/5/1982	81	FY1985	1991
Aircraft carrier	CVN-74	*John C. Stennis*	6/23/1988a	86	FY1988	1995
Sealift ship	TAKR-300	*Bob Hope*	1/27/1994	90	FY1993	1998
Aircraft carrier	CVN-76	*Ronald Reagan*	2/2/1995	83	FY1995	2003
Attack submarine	SSN-23	*Jimmy Carter*	4/8/1998	73	FY1996b	2005
Destroyer	DDG-94	*Nitze*	1/10/2001	93	FY1999	2005
Aircraft carrier	CVN-77	*George H.W. Bush*	12/9/2002	78	FY2001	2009
Destroyer	DDG-108	*Wayne E. Meyer*	11/29/2006	80	FY2004	2009
Attack submarine	SSN-785	*John Warner*	1/8/2009	81	FY2010	*2015*
Mobile Landing Platform Ship	MLP-2	*John Glenn*	1/4/2012	90	FY2011	*2014*
Littoral Combat Ship	LCS-10	*Gabrielle Giffords*	2/10/2012	41	FY2012	*2016*
Destroyer	DDG-116	*Thomas Hudner*	5/7/2012	87	FY2012	*2017*
Destroyer	DDG-117	*Paul Ignatius*	5/23/2013	92	FY2013	*2018*

Source: Compiled by CRS. Source for dates when names were announced for CVN-70 through DDG-108: Navy Office of Legislative Affairs email to CRS, May 1, 2012.

a.   This was the date that President Reagan announced that the ship would be named for Stennis. The Navy officially named the ship for Stennis on December 19, 1988.

b.   SSN-23 was originally procured in FY1992. Its procurement was suspended, and then reinstated in FY1996.

Public's Role in Naming Ships

Members of the public are sometimes interested in having Navy ships named for their own states or cities, for earlier U.S. Navy ships (particularly those on which they or their relatives served), for battles in which they or their relatives participated, or for people they admire. Citizens with such an interest sometimes contact the Navy, the Department of Defense, or Congress seeking support for their proposals. An October 2008 news report, for example, suggested that a letter-writing campaign by New Hampshire elementary school students that began in January 2004 was instrumental in the Navy's decision in August 2004 to name a Virginia-class submarine after the state.[45] The July 2012 Navy report to Congress states:

> In addition to receiving input and recommendations from the President and Congress, every Secretary of the Navy receives numerous requests from service members, citizens, interest groups, or individual members of Congress who want to name a ship in honor of a particular hometown, or State, or place, or hero, or famous ship. This means the "nomination" process is often fiercely contested as differing groups make the case that "their" ship name is the most fitting choice for a Secretary to make.[46]

---

[45] Dean Lohmeyer, "Students Who Helped Name the Navy's Newest Sub Tour State's Namesake," *Navy News Service*, October 25, 2008.

[46] Department of the Navy, *A Report on Policies and Practices of the U.S. Navy for Naming the Vessels of the Navy*, undated but transmitted to Congress with cover letters dated July 13, 2012, pp. 12-13.

Members of the public may also express their opposition to an announced naming decision. The July 2012 Navy report to Congress cites and discusses five recent examples of ship-naming decisions that were criticized by some observers: the destroyer DDG-1002 (named for President Lyndon Johnson), the Littoral Combat Ship LCS-10 (named for former Representative Gabrielle Giffords), the amphibious ship LPD-26 (named for late Representative John P. Murtha), the auxiliary ship TAKE-13 (named for Medgar Evers), and the auxiliary ship TAKE-14 (named for Cesar Chavez).[47]

Congress's Role in Naming Ships

Congressional Influence on Pending Navy Ship-Naming Decisions

Congress has long maintained an interest in how Navy ships are named,[48] and has influenced or may have influenced pending Navy decisions on the naming of certain ships, including but not limited to the following:

- One source states that "[the aircraft carriers] CVN 72 and CVN 73 were named prior to their start [of construction], in part to preempt potential congressional pressure to name one of those ships for Admiral H.G. Rickover ([instead,] the [attack submarine] SSN 709 was named for the admiral)."[49]

- There was a friendly rivalry of sorts in Congress between those who supported naming the aircraft carrier CVN-76 for President Truman and those who supported naming it for President Reagan; the issue was effectively resolved by a decision announced by President Clinton in February 1995 to name one carrier (CVN-75) for Truman and another (CVN-76) for Reagan.[50]

- One press report suggests that the decision to name CVN-77 for President George H. W. Bush may have been influenced by a congressional suggestion.[51]

- Section 1012 of the FY2007 John Warner National Defense Authorization Act (II.R. 5122/P.L. 109-364 of October 17, 2006), expressed the sense of the Congress that the aircraft carrier CVN-78 should be named for President Gerald R. Ford. The Navy announced on January 16, 2007, that CVN-78 would be named Gerald R. Ford.

---

[47] Department of the Navy, *A Report on Policies and Practices of the U.S. Navy for Naming the Vessels of the Navy*, undated but transmitted to Congress with cover letters dated July 13, 2012, p. 15.

[48] For example, the 1819 and 1858 laws cited in footnote 3 set forth naming rules for certain kinds of ships. Today, 10 U.S.C. §7292(b) still requires that battleships (which the United States has not built since World War II) be named after states.

[49] *The Naval Institute Guide to the Ships and Aircraft of the U.S. Fleet*, op cit, p. 113. See also p. 70 and p. 86.

[50] Patrick Pexton, "Clinton Compromise: Carriers Truman *And* Reagan," *Navy Times*, February 13, 1995: 19. See also "Navy Announces Aircraft Carrier To Be Named For President Truman," *Associated Press*, February 2, 1995. CVN-75 had been preliminarily named the United States.

[51] The article, which reported on the ship's official naming ceremony, states: "[Senator] Warner recalled that he first suggested naming a carrier in the senior Bush's honor last year [i.e., in 2001], during a ceremony in Newport News to christen the [previous] carrier Ronald Reagan." (Dale Eisman, "Navy Names New Aircraft Carrier For Elder Bush," *Norfolk Virginian-Pilot*, December 10, 2002.)

- In the 111th Congress, H.Res. 1505, introduced on July 1, 2010, expressed the sense of the House of Representatives that the Secretary of the Navy should name the next appropriate naval ship in honor of John William Finn. The measure was not acted on after being referred to the House Armed Services Committee. On February 15, 2012, the Navy announced that DDG-113, an Arleigh Burke (DDG-51) class destroyer, would be named *John Finn*.[52]

- Section 1012 of the FY2012 National Defense Authorization Act (H.R. 1540/P.L. 112-81 of December 31, 2011) expressed the sense of Congress that the Secretary of the Navy is encouraged to name the next available naval vessel after Rafael Peralta. On February 15, 2012, the Navy announced that DDG-113, an Arleigh Burke (DDG-51) class destroyer, would be named *Rafael Peralta*.[53]

The July 2012 Navy report to Congress states that

> every Secretary of the Navy, regardless of point of view [on how to name ships], is subject to a variety of outside influences when considering the best names to choose. The first among these comes from the President of the United States, under whose direction any Secretary works...

> Secretaries of the Navy must also consider the input of Congress.... Given the vital role Congress plays in maintaining the Navy-Marine Corps Team, any Secretary is sure to respect and consider its input when considering ships names.

> Sometimes, the Secretary must also balance or contend with differences of opinion between the President and Congress.[54]

The Navy suggests that congressional offices wishing to express support for proposals to name a Navy ship for a specific person, place, or thing contact the office of the Secretary of the Navy to make their support known. Congress may also pass legislation relating to ship names (see below).

Congressional Responses to Announced Navy Ship-Naming Decisions

Congress can pass legislation regarding a ship-naming decision that has been announced by the Navy. Such legislation can express Congress's views regarding the Navy's announced decision, and if Congress so desires, can also suggest or direct the Navy to take some action. The following are two examples of such legislation:

- **H.Res. 1022 of the 111th Congress** is an example of a measure reflecting support for an announced Navy ship-naming decision. This measure, introduced on January 20, 2010, and passed by the House on February 4, 2010, congratulates the Navy on its decision to name a naval ship for Medgar Evers.

---

[52] DOD News Release No. 109-12, February 15, 2012, entitled "Navy Names Five New Ships," accessed July 27, 2012, at http://www.defense.gov/releases/release.aspx?releaseid=15065.

[53] DOD News Release No. 109-12, February 15, 2012, entitled "Navy Names Five New Ships," accessed July 27, 2012, at http://www.defense.gov/releases/release.aspx?releaseid=15065.

[54] Department of the Navy, *A Report on Policies and Practices of the U.S. Navy for Naming the Vessels of the Navy*, undated but transmitted to Congress with cover letters dated July 13, 2012, pp. 11-12.

- **H.Con.Res. 312 of the 97ᵗʰ Congress** is an example of a measure that appears to reflect disagreement with an announced Navy ship-naming decision. This measure expressed the sense of Congress that the Los Angeles (SSN-688) class attack submarine *Corpus Christi* (SSN-705) should be renamed, and that a nonlethal naval vessel should instead be named *Corpus Christi*. (Los Angeles-class attack submarines were named for cities, and SSN-705 had been named for Corpus Christi, TX.) H.Con.Res. 312 was introduced on April 21, 1982, and was referred to the Seapower and Strategic and Critical Materials subcommittee of the House Armed Services Committee on April 28, 1982. On May 10, 1982, the Navy modified the name of SSN-705 to *City of Corpus Christi*.

An April 18, 2013, press release from Senator Angus King states:

> WASHINGTON, D.C. – U.S. Senators Susan Collins and Angus King today sent a letter to Ray Mabus, the Secretary of the Navy, asking that the USS Portland, a new San Antonio-class amphibious transport dock ship named after the city of Portland, Oregon, also be named in honor of Portland, Maine, consistent with the long history and tradition of U.S. Navy ships bestowed with the name USS Portland.
>
> Below is the full text of the letter:
>
> Dear Secretary Mabus:
>
> On April 12, 2013, you announced that LPD 27, a new San Antonio-class amphibious transport dock ship, will be named the USS Portland after the city of Portland, Oregon.
>
> We were surprised that the press release did not state that the ship was also named in honor of the city of Portland, Maine. We write to ask that you clarify that the ship will also be named in honor of Portland, Maine, consistent with the long history and tradition of U.S. Navy ships bestowed with the name USS Portland.
>
> The Department of the Navy press release stated LPD 27 will be the third ship to bear the name USS Portland. The press release failed to mention that both of the previous two ships were named, in whole or in part, to honor the city of Portland, Maine. The first USS Portland (CA-33) was the lead ship of a new class of heavy cruisers. Launched in 1932, it was named after the city of Portland, Maine, and saw battle during World War II at the 1942 Battle of the Coral Sea, the Battle of Midway, and the Battle of Guadalcanal. After accruing 16 battle stars, she was decommissioned in 1946.
>
> The second USS Portland (LSD-37) was commissioned in 1970 and served until 2004. The ship was also named after the city of Portland, Maine, but it was also named after the city of Portland, Oregon. The ship's insignia incorporates the seals of both cities.
>
> The third USS Portland should continue this tradition. We understand that amphibious transport dock ships are named for major American cities, and we can assure you that Portland, Maine is the largest city in Maine and the metro area is home to one-third of Maine's entire population.
>
> Portland also has a rich naval history. South Portland is where many Liberty cargo ships were built that sustained the war effort during World War II, and 4,700 skilled shipyard workers repair Los Angeles-class and Virginia-class nuclear powered submarines one hour to the south of Portland at the Portsmouth Naval Shipyard. Portland also has the largest port in Maine, and it is home to men and women whose livelihood relies upon the ocean and its resources, as demonstrated by the historic and bustling working waterfront.

We are confident that the impressive capabilities of LPD 27 and her crew can honor Portland, Maine, without in any way reducing the simultaneous honor afforded to Portland, Oregon. In fact, part of the rich history of Portland, Oregon, is that it was named after the city in Maine. In 1845, two of the city's founders, Asa Lovejoyof Boston, and Francis Pettygroveof Portland, Maine, each wanted to name the new city after his original home town. After Pettygrove won a coin toss two out of three times, the city was named after Portland, Maine. You can view the "Portland Penny" in person at the Oregon Historical Society in downtown Portland, Oregon.

We request that you clarify that the USS Portland will be named in honor of Portland, Maine, as well as Portland, Oregon. Given the history of both cities and the previous ships given the proud name of USS Portland, we are confident that you will agree that doing so will greatly contribute to the rich and storied history the USS Portland will carry with her as she and her crew defend our nation.[55]

Past Legislation on Naming Ships

Table 2 shows recent enacted provisions regarding the names of Navy ships. All of these measures expressed the sense of the Congress (or of the Senate or House) about how a Navy ship should be named.

---

[55] Press release accessed on April 26, 2013, at http://www.king.senate.gov/record.cfm?id=341463. For a press report, see Associated Press, "Navy Asked To Fix Snub Of Portland In Ship's Name," *Boston Globe*, April 20, 2013.

Table 2. Recent Enacted Legislative Provisions

Fiscal Year	Public Law	Bill	Section	Ship	Name(s)
2013	P.L. 113-6	H.R. 933	8119 of Division C	the next available capital warship	*Ted Stevens*
2012	P.L. 112-81	H.R. 1540	1012	the next available naval vessel	*Rafael Peralta*
2011	P.L. 111-383	H.R. 6523	1022	a combat vessel	*Father Vincent Capodanno*
2007	P.L. 109-364	H.R. 5122	1012	CVN-78	*Gerald R. Ford*
2001	P.L. 106-398	H.R. 4205	1012	CVN-77	*Lexington*
1999	P.L. 105-261	H.R. 3616	1014	an LPD-17 class ship	*Clifton B. Cates*
1996	P.L. 104-106	S. 1124	1018	LHD-7	*Iwo Jima*
1996	P.L. 104-106	S. 1124	1018	LPD-17 class amphibious ships	*Marine Corps battles or members of Marine Corps*
1996	P.L. 104-106	S. 1124	1019	an appropriate ship	*Joseph Vittori*
1991	P.L. 101-510	H.R. 4739	1426	the next DDG-51	*Samuel S. Stratton*
1989	P.L. 100-456	H.R. 4481	1221	the next SSBN	*Melvin Price*
1989	P.L. 100-456	H.R. 4481	1222	an appropriate ship	*Bob Hope*
1989	P.L. 100-202	H.J.Res. 395	8138	CVN-74 or CVN-75	*John C. Stennis*

Source: Prepared by CRS. All of these provisions expressed the sense of the Congress (or of the Senate or House) about how a Navy ship should be named.

Table 3 shows examples of proposed bills and amendments regarding the names of Navy ships going back to the 93rd Congress. Some of these measures expressed the sense of the Congress about how a Navy ship should be named, while others would mandate a certain name for a ship. Although few of these measures were acted on after being referred to committee, they all signaled congressional interest in how certain ships should be named, and thus may have influenced Navy decisions on these matters.

Table 3. Examples of Proposed Bills and Amendments

[Congress] and Bill	Ship	Proposed name(s)
[112th] H.Con.Res. 48	a Littoral Combat Ship	*Ypsilanti*
[112th] H.R. 1945	next available naval vessel	*Rafael Peralta*
[111th] H.Res. 1505	next appropriate naval ship	*John William Finn*
[111th] H.Res. 330	an appropriate ship	*Clifton B. Cates*
[111th] H.Con.Res. 83	CVN-79 or CVN-80	*Barry M. Goldwater*
[109th] S. 2766	CVN-78	*Gerald R. Ford*
[107th] H.Con.Res. 294	a new naval vessel	*Bluejacket*
[106th] S.Con.Res. 84	CVN-77	*Lexington*
[105th] S.Amdt. 2812 to S. 2057	LPD-17 class ship	*Clifton B. Cates*
[104th] H.J.Res. 61	CVN-76	*Ronald Reagan*
[104th] H.R. 445	CVN-76	*Harry Truman*
[104th] S.Con.Res. 62	SSN-774	*South Dakota*
[104th] S.J.Res. 17	CVN-76	*Ronald Reagan*
[104th] S.Amdt. 2277 to S. 1026	LHD-7	*Iwo Jima*
[104th] S.Amdt. 2277 to S. 1026	LPD-17 class ships	famous Marine Corps battles or heroes
[104th] S.Amdt. 4350 to S. 1745	a SSN-774 class submarine	*South Dakota*
[103rd] H.R. 5283	an appropriate ship	*Joseph Vittori*
[102nd] H.Con.Res. 354	a guided missile cruiser	*Pearl Harbor*
[102nd] H.R. 6115	CVN-76	*Harry S Truman*
[100th] H.Amdt. 614 to H.R. 4264	next SSBN-726 class submarine deployed after enactment	*Melvin Price*
[100th] S.Amdt. 1354 to H.J.Res. 395	CVN-74 or CVN-75	*John C. Stennis*
[98th] H.Res. 99	an aircraft carrier	*Wasp*
[97th] H.Con.Res. 312	a nonlethal naval vessel[a]	*Corpus Christi*[a]
[97th] H.Res. 174	an aircraft carrier	*Wasp*
[97th] H.R. 4977	CVN-72	*Hyman G. Rickover*
[93rd] H.Con.Res. 386	CVN-70	*Carl Vinson*
[93rd] H.Con.Res. 387	CVN-70	*Carl Vinson*
[93rd] H.J.Res. 831	CVN-70	*Carl Vinson*

Source: Prepared by CRS.

a. H.Con.Res. 312 expressed the sense of Congress that the Los Angeles (SSN-688) class attack submarine *Corpus Christi* (SSN-705) should be renamed, and that a nonlethal naval vessel should instead be named *Corpus Christi*. (Los Angeles-class attack submarines were named for cities, and SSN-705 had been named for Corpus Christi, TX.) H.Con.Res. 312 was introduced on April 21, 1982, and was referred to the Seapower and Strategic and Critical Materials subcommittee of the House Armed Services Committee on April 28, 1982. On May 10, 1982, the Navy changed the name of SSN-705 to *City of Corpus Christi*.

Legislative Activity in 113th Congress

H.R. 933/P.L. 113-6 (Consolidated and Further Continuing Appropriations Act, 2013)

H.R. 933 as passed by the Senate on March 20, 2013, and the House on March 21, 2013, was signed into law as P.L. 113-6 on March 26, 2013. The act includes the FY2013 DOD appropriations act as Division C. Section 8119 of Division C states:

> Sec. 8119. It is the Sense of the Senate that the next available capital warship of the U.S. Navy be named the USS Ted Stevens to recognize the public service achievements, military service sacrifice, and undaunted heroism and courage of the long-serving United States Senator for Alaska.

Appendix A. Executive Summary of July 2012 Navy Report to Congress

This appendix reprints the executive summary of the July 2012 Navy report to Congress on the Navy's policies and practices for naming its ships. The text of the executive summary is as follows:

Executive Summary

This report is submitted in accordance with Section 1014 of P.L. 112-81, National Defense Authorization Act (NDAA) for Fiscal Year 2012, dated 31 December 2011, which directs the Secretary of Defense to submit a report on "policies and practices of the Navy for naming vessels of the Navy."

As required by the NDAA, this report:

- Includes a description of the current policies and practices of the Navy for naming vessels of the Navy, and a description of the extent to which theses policies and practices vary from historical policies and practices of the Navy for naming vessels of the Navy, and an explanation for such variances;

- Assesses the feasibility and advisability of establishing fixed policies for the naming of one or more classes of vessels of the Navy, and a statement of the policies recommended to apply to each class of vessels recommended to be covered by such fixed policies if the establishment of such fixed policies is considered feasible and advisable; and

- Identifies any other matter relating to the policies and practices of the Navy for naming vessels of the Navy that the Secretary of Defense considers appropriate.

After examining the historical record in great detail, this report concludes:

- Current ship naming policies and practices fall well within the historic spectrum of policies and practices for naming vessels of the Navy, and are altogether consistent with ship naming customs and traditions.

- The establishment of fixed policies for the naming of one or more classes of vessels of the Navy would be highly inadvisable. There is no objective evidence to suggest that fixed policies would improve Navy ship naming policies and practices, which have worked well for over two centuries.

In addition, the Department of the Navy used to routinely publish lists of current type naming conventions for battle force ships, and update it as changes were made to them. At some point, this practice fell into disuse, leading to a general lack of knowledge about naming conventions. To remedy this problem, the Naval History and Heritage Command will once again develop and publish a list of current type naming conventions to help all Americans better understand why Secretaries of the Navy choose the ship names they do. This list will be updated as required.[56]

---

[56] Department of the Navy, *A Report on Policies and Practices of the U.S. Navy for Naming the Vessels of the Navy*, (continued...)

Appendix B. Legislative Activity in 112th Congress

H.R. 4310/P.L. 112-239 (FY2013 National Defense Authorization Act)

Senate

On December 3, 2012, as part of its consideration of the FY2013 National Defense Authorization Act (S. 3254), the Senate agreed to by voice vote S.Amdt. 3054, the text of which is as follows:

> Sec. 1024. NOTICE TO CONGRESS AND WAIT ON PROPOSALS TO NAME NAVAL VESSELS.
>
> Section 7292 of title 10, United States Code, is amended by adding at the end the following new subsection:
>
> "(d) The Secretary of the Navy may not announce or implement any proposal to name a vessel of the Navy until 30 days after the date on which the Secretary submits to the Committees on Armed Services of the Senate and the House of Representatives a report setting forth such proposal.".

Conference

Section 1018 of the conference report (H.Rept. 112-705 of December 18, 2012) on H.R. 4310/P.L. 112-239 of January 2, 2013, states:

> SEC. 1018. NOTICE TO CONGRESS FOR THE REVIEW OF PROPOSALS TO NAME NAVAL VESSELS.
>
> (a) FINDINGS.—Congress makes the following findings:
>
> (1) The Navy traces its ancestry to October 13, 1775, when an Act of the Continental Congress authorized the first vessel of a navy for the United Colonies. Vessels of the Continental Navy were named for early patriots and military heroes, Federal institutions, colonial cities, and positive character traits representative of naval and military virtues.
>
> (2) An Act of Congress on March 3, 1819, made the Secretary of the Navy responsible for assigning names to vessels of the Navy. Traditional sources for vessel names customarily encompassed such categories as geographic locations in the United States; historic sites, battles, and ships; naval and military heroes and leaders; and noted individuals who made distinguished contributions to United States national security.
>
> (3) These customs and traditions provide appropriate and necessary standards for the naming of vessels of the Navy.
>
> (b) NOTICE TO CONGRESS.—Section 7292 of title 10, United States Code, is amended by adding at the end the following new subsection:

(...continued)

undated but transmitted to Congress with cover letters dated July 13, 2012, p. iii.

"(d)(1) The Secretary of the Navy may not announce or implement any proposal to name a vessel of the Navy until 30 days after the date on which the Secretary submits to the Committees on Armed Services of the Senate and the House of Representatives a report setting forth such proposal.

"(2) Each report under this subsection shall describe the justification for the proposal covered by such report in accordance with the standards referred to in section 1024(a) of the National Defense Authorization Act for Fiscal Year 2013.".

(c) EFFECTIVE DATE.—This section and the amendment made by this section shall go into effect on the date that is 30 days after the date of the enactment of this Act.

Regarding Section 1018, the Joint Explanatory Statement for the conference report states:

The Senate amendment contained a provision (sec. 1024) that would identify appropriate and necessary standards for the naming of vessels of the Navy, and would amend section 7292 of title 10, United States Code, by adding a new subsection that would prevent the Secretary of the Navy from announcing or implementing any proposal to name a vessel of the Navy until 30 days after the date on which the Secretary submits to the Committees on Armed Services of the Senate and the House of Representatives a report that justifies how such a naming proposal follows the appropriate and necessary standards for the naming of vessels of the Navy set forth in this Act.

The House bill contained no similar provision.

The House recedes.

The conferees agree that: (1) the ship naming process must not be politicized; (2) setting forth objective criteria can help in this goal; and (3) establishing a notify-and-wait period will aid the Armed Service Committees' oversight of the process. (Pages 201-202)

H.R. 5856 (FY2013 DOD Appropriations Act)

Senate

Section 8111 of H.R. 5856 as reported by the Senate Appropriations Committee (S.Rept. 112-196 of August 2, 2012) states:

Sec. 8111. It is the Sense of the Senate that the next available capital warship of the U.S. Navy be named the USS Ted Stevens to recognize the public service achievements, military service sacrifice, and undaunted heroism and courage of the long-serving United States Senator for Alaska.

Conference

For further action on H.R. 5856 of the 112th Congress, see H.R. 933 of the 113th Congress in "Legislative Activity of 113th Congress."

H.R. 1540/P.L. 112-81 (FY2012 National Defense Authorization Act)

Senate (S. 1867)

On November 30, 2011, as part of its consideration of the FY2012 National Defense Authorization Act (S. 1867),[57] the Senate adopted an en bloc amendment that included, among other things, S.Amdt. 1134. The text of S.Amdt. 1134 is as follows:

> At the end of subtitle C of title X, add the following:
>
> SEC. 1024. REPORT ON POLICIES AND PRACTICES OF THE NAVY FOR NAMING THE VESSELS OF THE NAVY.
>
> (a) Report Required.—Not later than 180 days after the date of the enactment of this Act, the Secretary of Defense shall submit to Congress a report on the policies and practices of the Navy for naming vessels of the Navy.
>
> (b) Elements.—The report required by subsection (a) shall set forth the following:
>
> (1) A description of the current policies and practices of the Navy for naming vessels of the Navy.
>
> (2) A description of the extent to which the policies and practices described under paragraph (1) vary from historical policies and practices of the Navy for naming vessels of the Navy, and an explanation for such variances (if any).
>
> (3) An assessment of the feasibility and advisability of establishing fixed policies for the naming of one or more classes of vessels of the Navy, and a statement of the policies recommended to apply to each class of vessels recommended to be covered by such fixed policies if the establishment of such fixed policies is considered feasible and advisable.
>
> (4) Any other matters relating to the policies and practices of the Navy for naming vessels of the Navy that the Secretary of Defense considers appropriate.

Conference (H.R. 1540)

In the conference report (H.Rept. 112-329 of December 12, 2011) on H.R. 1540/P.L. 112-81 of December 31, 2011, the text of **Section 1012** is as follows:

> SEC. 1012. SENSE OF CONGRESS ON NAMING OF NAVAL VESSEL AFTER UNITED STATES MARINE CORPS SERGEANT RAFAEL PERALTA.
>
> It is the sense of Congress that the Secretary of the Navy is encouraged to name the next available Naval vessel after United States Marine Corps Sergeant Rafael Peralta.

(See also H.R. 1945, discussed below.)

The text of **Section 1014** of H.R. 1540 is as follows:

---

[57] S. 1867, an original measure reported by Senator Levin on November 15, 2011, without written report, in effect superseded S. 1253, an earlier version of the FY2012 National Defense Authorization Act.

SEC. 1014. REPORT ON POLICIES AND PRACTICES OF THE NAVY FOR NAMING THE VESSELS OF THE NAVY.

(a) Report Required- Not later than 180 days after the date of the enactment of this Act, the Secretary of Defense shall submit to Congress a report on the policies and practices of the Navy for naming vessels of the Navy.

(b) Elements- The report required by subsection (a) shall set forth the following:

(1) A description of the current policies and practices of the Navy for naming vessels of the Navy.

(2) A description of the extent to which the policies and practices described under paragraph (1) vary from historical policies and practices of the Navy for naming vessels of the Navy, and an explanation for such variances (if any).

(3) An assessment of the feasibility and advisability of establishing fixed policies for the naming of one or more classes of vessels of the Navy, and a statement of the policies recommended to apply to each class of vessels recommended to be covered by such fixed policies if the establishment of such fixed policies is considered feasible and advisable.

(4) Any other matters relating to the policies and practices of the Navy for naming vessels of the Navy that the Secretary of Defense

H.Con.Res. 48 (Regarding Naming a Littoral Combat Ship for Ypsilanti, Michigan)

The text of H.Con.Res. 48, introduced on May 4, 2011, is as follows:

CONCURRENT RESOLUTION

Expressing the sense of Congress that the Secretary of the Navy should name a Littoral Combat Ship the U.S.S. Ypsilanti, in honor of Ypsilanti, Michigan.

Whereas the Navy proposes the procurement of 55 Littoral Combats Ships;

Whereas the Navy has stated it will name Littoral Combats Ships for small towns and communities and mid-size cities;

Whereas the City of Ypsilanti and Ypsilanti Township, Michigan, with a combined population of 74,439, is a small city that satisfies the criteria for naming Littoral Combats Ships;

Whereas Ypsilanti, Michigan, is named in honor of General Demetrius Ypsilanti, who is considered a Greek war hero for his contributions to achieving Greece's independence in 1829;

Whereas in 1829, the Michigan settlement of Woodruff's Grove combined land acquired by three prominent settlers and changed its name to the City of Ypsilanti;

Whereas Ypsilanti is located in the county that hosts the only Naval Reserve Officer Training Corps unit in Michigan;

Whereas the NROTC unit prepares students from Eastern Michigan University, located in Ypsilanti, for service as officers in both the United States Navy and the United States Marine Corps; and

Whereas the Littoral Combats Ships are designed to operate in littoral, or close-to-shore environments, and a Navy vessel the bearing the name U.S.S. Ypsilanti would help convey the American ideals of freedom and democracy to nations struggling to achieve democracy: Now, therefore, be it

Resolved by the House of Representatives (the Senate concurring), That it is the sense of Congress that the Secretary of the Navy should name a Littoral Combat Ship in honor of Ypsilanti, Michigan.

H.R. 1945 (Regarding Naming A Naval Vessel For Rafael Peralta)

The text of H.R. 1945, introduced on May 23, 2011, is as follows:

A BILL

To direct the Secretary of the Navy to name the next available Naval vessel after United States Marine Corps Sergeant Rafael Peralta.

Be it enacted by the Senate and House of Representatives of the United States of America in Congress assembled,

SECTION 1. NAMING OF NAVAL VESSEL AFTER UNITED STATES MARINE CORPS SERGEANT RAFAEL PERALTA.

The Secretary of the Navy shall name the next available Naval vessel after United States Marine Corps Sergeant Rafael Peralta.

H.Rept. 112-88 of May 24, 2011, which provided for the further consideration of H.R. 1540, the FY2012 National Defense Authorization Act, listed an amendment (No. 36) similar in purpose to H.R. 1945.[58] H.Rept. 112-88 stated that this amendment

Would encourage the Secretary of the Navy to name the next available ship after Marine Corps Sergeant Rafael Peralta. Sergeant Peralta, who grew up in Southeast San Diego, was nominated for the Medal of Honor for smothering a grenade with his body during combat in Fallujah, Iraq. He was posthumously awarded the Navy Cross instead. A team of specialists, which included pathologists and other experts, conducted an investigation at the direction of the Secretary of Defense and determined that Peralta did not consciously pull the grenade into his body. This conclusion contradicts the eye-witness accounts of the Marines fighting alongside Peralta, as well as the recommendation put forward by Marine Corps leadership. There have been 11 instances, going back to 1989, where Congress has included in legislation that was signed into law how a Navy ship should be named. (Pages 6-7)

---

[58] H.Rept. 112-88, pages 47-48, states that amendment No. 36 would add a new section to H.R. 1540 as follows:

SEC. 1022. NAMING OF NAVAL VESSEL AFTER UNITED STATES MARINE CORPS SERGEANT RAFAEL PERALTA.

Congress strongly encourages the Secretary of the Navy to name the next available Naval vessel after United States Marine Corps Sergeant Rafael Peralta.

The Legislative Information System suggests that the House did not consider this amendment as part of its consideration of H.R. 1540 on May 24-26, 2011.

(See also §1012 of H.R. 1540/P.L. 112-81, discussed above.)

Author Contact Information

Ronald O'Rourke
Specialist in Naval Affairs
rorourke@crs.loc.gov, 7-7610